Sugar & Spice

by
R.E. Hargrave

Sugar & Spice

**Copyright © 2013 R.E. Hargrave
2nd Edition
All rights reserved.
ISBN-10: 1495379175
ISBN-13: 978-1495379178**

R.E. Hargrave

2nd Edition Published by R.E. Hargrave
Copyright R.E. Hargrave 2013

The right of R.E. Hargrave to be identified as the author of this work has been asserted by her under the Copyright Amendment (Moral Rights) Act 2000

License Notes: This novella is licensed for your personal enjoyment only. This print may not be re-sold or given away to other people. If you would like to share this book with another person, please purchase an additional copy for each recipient. If you're reading this book and did not purchase it, or it was not purchased for your use only, then please purchase your own copy. Thank you for respecting the hard work of this author.

This book is a work of fiction and any resemblance to persons, living or dead, or places, events or locales is purely coincidental. The characters are productions of the author's imagination and used fictitiously.

This work is copyright. Apart from any use as permitted under the Copyright Act 1968, no part may be reproduced, copied, scanned, stored in a retrieval system, recorded or transmitted, in any form or by any means, without the prior written permission of the publisher.

Cover design by: J.C. Clarke
Cover image: © David Coleman-Dreamstime.com; © stockcreations-Dreamstime.com

Acknowledgements

Thank You ~
To my husband for putting up with the hours wiled away at the computer and all the times you did the grocery shopping in my stead.

To my children — Nathaniel, Nicholas and Meredith — thank you for making me proud and being such great kids.

To everyone who has been my guinea pig in the last couple of years while I tried different styles, it was your words of encouragement that helped me find the courage to take this leap.

Thank you, Tammy, for the adorable yet stylish cover.

Thank you Tammy, Mich, Judy, and Massy for helping me keep my plot in line; with a shout out to Elizabeth M. Lawrence for editing!

And lastly, an extra special thank you to my own precocious nine-year-old, who was the best pre-reader and character inspiration a gal could have asked for on this project. I love you, Norbert.

R.E. Hargrave

Table of Contents

Acknowledgements 4
Chapter 1 6
Chapter 2 19
Chapter 3 28
Chapter 4 39
Chapter 5 49
Chapter 6 57
Chapter 7 65
Chapter 8 74
Chapter 9 84
Chapter 10 93
Chapter 11 105
Epilogue 116
About the Author 117

Chapter 1
~February~

Sugar and spice and all things nice. That's what little girls are made of! ~Mother Goose

Running down my ingredient list in my mind, I pushed the grocery cart towards the back section of the store to where the eggs were kept. I needed five dozen; then I could be on my way back to the bakery up the street. Sugar & Spice was small, but it was mine—all that I had besides my daughter Candace, who would be ten in August.

Her father had been my first, and last, crush. A dashing senior, Mark Reynolds had been the star quarterback at Union High School. I became smitten with him when I was a sixteen-year-old junior. I'd been entranced by his bright blue eyes and easy smile, which were always framed by his shaggy brown hair, and his carefree approach to life—it seemed when he smiled, things fell into place for him. Case in point: when he showed signs of struggling in History, a smile was all it took for me to offer my help. Over time, those study sessions drifted into make out sessions, and then more.

He'd seemed so sweet to my naïve self. I never questioned it when he suggested that we meet at the old library downtown—I thought he had an honest concern about the noise volume. I understood when he had practice or a game and didn't have time for "real" dates. It was exciting when he'd drive me home from the library, taking the long route through the park. In the back of my mind, I'd known his touches should not have been so exploratory, but they made me feel alive. Or so I'd thought at the time.

Our so-called relationship had continued, with secret touches in the hallways and stolen kisses under the bleachers in the spare moments before practice—kisses that always had me melting under his spell and left me blind to his rough dismissals when he'd tell me I would distract him if I stayed to watch. That spell had been shattered when I started experiencing flu symptoms that wouldn't go away, and my father took me to the doctor. Imagine both of our surprise when the doctor had come in with the news that I was going to be a mommy.

At first, my father had been crushed, thinking he had failed in raising me on his own. He berated himself, his ramblings of self-loathing revealed to me the true story behind my mother's absence. In her opinion, she had been too young. She hadn't thought motherhood was for her—a decision she'd made in the middle of the night when I was four months old. That was the last time we'd seen or heard from her.

However, once he'd had a couple of days to calm down, my father was prepared to stand at my side and help me get through it—starting with the visit to let Mark know he was going to be a daddy.

Arriving at Mark's house, his mom had been a little confused because she didn't know about us, a fact that had been dumbfounding – I couldn't believe Mark had never spoken of me – but she'd been polite and invited us in anyway. We'd been making pleasant conversation regarding the various activities happening at school when Mark arrived home from the gym. I had caught the way his eyes had widened in surprise, and I knew in that moment that I'd been nothing more than a dirty little secret to him—good enough to woo into bed, but not good enough be "together" in public. Despite Mark's protestations that he didn't know me as anything beyond a fellow schoolmate, my father had pressed forward and dropped the bomb.

Mark had denied it, and his mother had supported him. He had a full ride to Notre Dame on a football scholarship, and she was not going to let his future be ruined because of his promiscuous inclinations. This had angered my father to the point that he made Mark sign a statement waiving any claim to parental rights. Daddy didn't want any trouble from him later on over custody. That had been January, and I'd been almost three months along.

With my father's love and support, I'd finished out my junior year, determined to make something of myself in spite of my situation. I refused to let it ruin my life or that of my unborn child. My belly grew more each month, along with the whispers and stares from my classmates and some of the ladies from church. I ignored them all, stopped going to church, and disappeared into my love of baking, which had been born when I was five and Daddy had gotten me an Easy

Bake Oven. Daddy would take the surplus of the baked goods out to the Royal Hills Nursing Home. His job title there was head groundskeeper; in reality, he was also maintenance, chauffeur, and friend to most of the residents.

Candace Michelle Harrison was born on the fifteenth of August, giving me just enough time to make a physical recovery before my senior year started. Thanks to Daddy's relationship with them, the ladies at Royal Hills viewed me as a daughter and were more than happy to be stand-in doting grandmothers. They loved helping to keep an eye on Candy during the day while I attended classes.

The situation may have been unconventional, but it had worked. Our Royal Hills family had even gone so far as to pool their meager resources to give me the first year's lease on the shop as a graduation present, so certain were they that I had a future in baking. The gesture had left me a teary mess. I hadn't made a fortune off the shop, but Candy and I were comfortable almost ten years later and to this day, I brought a box of assorted goodies over to the home every week for my Sunday visit with the residents and dinner with Daddy.

R.E. Hargrave

It had been a quaint life in the small, rural South Carolina town of Union. Candy and I had a simple three-bedroom house with a small fenced-in backyard, which had allowed her to run around and play as a toddler and now gave her a quiet place to read and study as she grew. Running the bakery kept me busy most of the day, so I was unable to be as active in her school life as I would've liked. One thing I always made time for were the holiday PTA bake sales that were the school's biggest fundraiser. People came from the surrounding counties when we held our sales. Everything was handmade fresh by the moms, teachers, and students of Union Elementary in the Sugar and Spice kitchen.

This was why I was at the store with a cart full of flour, sugar, butter, shaved coconut, chocolate chips, assorted nuts, flavored extracts, and anything else you could need for a massive Valentine's Day bake-fest. While all the bake sales did well, the Valentine's and Christmas ones were our big money makers.

I had just piled up the last five flats of eggs from the cooler and was turning to put them into the cart when, without any warning, I collided with someone and found myself wearing five dozen eggs.

"Oh, my goodness, miss! I'm so sorry! Here, let me help ya," came a rich voice with a slight southern twang to it. Whoever it was, he wasn't a local—that was for sure. I felt the cartons being lifted away and paper towels being pressed into my hands, so I used the towels to wipe the egg off my face.

"Thanks," I managed to get out as I wiped at the egg bits around my chin, trying to avoid getting any in my mouth. With my face somewhat cleaned, I looked up into the amused azure eyes of my would-be assailant.

"Trent," he introduced himself with an outstretched hand; his other hand held a bouquet of beautiful daisies.

"Lacey," I replied. I was unable to keep the nerves out of my voice as I teased, "The flowers aren't necessary; this will clean up easy enough." I'd come a long way with my self-esteem and could now admit that I was good looking with my grassy eyes and raven-black hair cut in an attractive swing bob, but I continued to be wary of physical advances from men. You could say that Mark had ruined my ability to trust in men in general—except for Daddy, of course.

"Well, Lacey, it's nice to meet you. Let me apologize again by offering to pay for the broken eggs," he said.

We shared an awkward chuckle, and I was tempted. My usual routine was to donate the supplies for the bake sales since I didn't buy any of the finished products to take home. It was ironic that while I loved to bake, I did not have a sweet tooth. That was the most probable reason why I was still in a size ten. The supply donation was the whole reason I was at the grocery store in the first place; it was easier to do a separate store run and have a dedicated receipt rather than using business supplies and having to sort out the tax mess.

Before I could answer, his eyes took in the contents of my cart, and he got a quizzical look on his face.

"Got some baking to do?" he joked and flashed a smile that tugged at my insides.

"You could say that," I started. "The school bake sale is next week, and I always oversee the baking. Everyone is meeting at my shop now to get started."

"So this is a fundraiser?"

I nodded and grinned at him. "Most popular one for counties around," I announced with pride.

"Well, in that case, I insist on paying for the lot. Ya know, to show my support for the community and all," he said with a wink.

I found myself giggling like some featherbrained young girl. "That's a mighty fine offer, Trent, but how about you plan on coming out to the sale and putting your money on the finished treats?" I counter-offered. I think I was flirting with him, though I shouldn't have been. Chances were, given the flowers he was holding, he was attached to someone.

Trent was hard to ignore with his rugged handsomeness. His skin was tanned, a dusting of blonde scruff covered his jaw and chin, and he was muscled underneath his tee shirt and jeans, but his eyes—his eyes held the same rare kindness that I'd never seen in any other man except my father.

Something told me I was in trouble when I arrived back at the shop to the PTA ladies and their whispered gossip.

"Have you seen the new guy in town?"

"Isn't he dreamy?"

"Do you think he's single?"

"Yes, yes, and I'm not sure," I squealed, and all eyes landed on me seconds before the demands for me to spill began. Once I had changed into a spare, non-eggy set of chef pants and a tee, the rest of the afternoon was spent dissecting my encounter with the ladies gathered in my kitchen. The hours ticked away while the cooling trays filled with all manner of cookies, breads, and miniature cakes.

~oOo~

I made the drive from the grocery store out to Royal Hills with a dopey smile on my face. The woman I'd bumped into at the Food Lion had been an absolute delight. When I saw the smashed eggs dripping down her face and her green eyes blazing, the first word that popped into my head was "adorable." I needed to know more about her. Parking my car, I retrieved my bags, and headed for the door.

"Afternoon, Mr. Childress," a voice called from my right.

"Howdy, Mr. Harrison. Hedges are looking great," I called, shifting my body in the gardener's direction and slowing my walk. "Mom behave today?" I asked, and he tipped his hat.

"Yup, she didn't try harvesting my asters today," he replied with a chuckle, and I shook my head. Of course she went after those plants; they reminded her of the flowers she loved so much. Dad had courted her with wild daisies, and they'd been her favorite ever since. Since he'd passed and I had relocated here to be close by, I was doing my best to make sure she had fresh flowers every week.

I gave Mr. Harrison a wave and made my way inside to Mom's room, where I found her watching the bird houses that hung outside her window. A pair of hummingbirds was flitting back and forth, and I could see her blue eyes dance while she watched. Her hair was fixed in a neat bun; no longer the honey gold it had been in her youth, it was now a sophisticated silver.

"Hey, Mom," I said, loud enough for her to hear me, but not so loud that it would startle her. I waited a few moments, knowing she would soon turn and give me a welcoming smile.

"Trent!" she cried with surprised excitement, and I squelched the feeling inside—the knowledge that this was going to be one of those days when she would again ask the questions I hated answering. It killed me each time I had to tell her Dad was gone. Her doctor hadn't yet diagnosed her with Alzheimer's, though the indications all pointed to it. Her brief moments of lucidity made me question if her continual lapses in memory were intentional attempts to block her reality—if it was easier for her to exist in denial.

"I brought you some flowers and contraband chocolate," I played with her, handing over the daisies and the little three-pack of Toblerone.

"Such a sweet boy to remember his momma's favorites. Now if you'd just visit me and Pops more often, I'd be a happy woman," she proclaimed. Rather than tell her I'd been here just the day before, I told her about meeting Lacey.

Mom couldn't, or wouldn't, remember that I came by every day or that Dad was dead, but it soon became clear that she had no trouble recalling the magic that Lacey worked in her kitchen. I couldn't blame Mom for remembering the baker when she'd forgotten so many other things. Lacey had grown up here; I hadn't. Further, Lacey had been a regular part of Mom's life, or at least her baked goods had, since Mom had taken up residence at Royal Hills. I had been the long-distance son.

Listening to her talk about the treats which came from Lacey's kitchen each week served to prove that there was something special about Lacey, and Mom was delighted to hear she'd caught my eye. This, at least, was a story I wasn't going to mind retelling.

Two days later at the bake sale, I didn't hesitate to buy way too many goodies. Straightaway, I delivered them to the residents of Royal Hills, wishing them all a Happy Valentine's Day.

Chapter 2
~March~

The bells over the door chimed, causing me to glance at the clock and smile. That would be Candy getting in after her first day back to school following spring break. I loved her, but the past week with her underfoot in the kitchen hadn't been as relaxing as it had in years past. Also, it left me feeling a little sad. Every day, she seemed to get a bit older, while I wanted her to stay my baby girl forever. She was my daughter, but she was also my best friend. I walked a two-way street with her, relishing those proud moments when she accomplished something on her own, yet lamenting them as well.

Candy had always been my helper, eager to learn how to temper chocolate and fold ingredients into light and airy batters, excited to try her hand at frosting the cupcakes, curious about creating something new — until this year. This year, she had talked my ear off, chattering about the latest boy band, what the girls were wearing at school, and how she didn't have the same things. All the while she stood off to the side, thumbing through her teeny-bopper magazines that she kept convincing my father to buy for her. I felt like my little girl was already slipping away at just nine years old. I was losing her to her burgeoning independence, and now I had to accept the idea that she was going to grow up and leave. My time with her was limited, and then I would be left alone. I had no intentions of taking a single moment with her for granted.

"Mom!"

"In the back," I called out, not taking my attention off the icing I was battling at present, trying to get it the perfect shade of green for the four-leaf clover cookies that were cooling. They were my famous sugar cookies; always the same recipe, just a different presentation, depending on the event. The current occasion happened to be St. Patrick's Day.

Candy's arms came around me in a quick hug.

"No more cookies after that one, missy," I laughed, knowing she had snuck one from the cooling rack. "So, how was the first day back?"

Candy moved to the corner table I'd set up so she could do her homework after school and pulled out a math book. Her silence made me set down the food coloring and spoon and turn to face her. I'd never seen such a big grin on her face.

"That good, huh?"

"Uh-huh," she sang back and twirled a loop of her long hair around her finger. In normal light, it was black like mine, but when the sun hit it as an errant ray was doing now, you could see flashes of auburn strands — a lingering gift from her father. We'd both had green eyes, so neither one of us could claim Candy's blue ones, though Daddy said my mother had blue eyes. I was grateful that other than her eyes and the lighter hair color, she looked more like me than her biological father.

"So, are you going to elaborate?" I asked, grabbing a cookie and spreading a dab of the frosting on it as a bribe to get her to talk. She took the cookie, blowing me a kiss, while I went to get her a glass of milk.

"Coach went into labor the first day of break—" she started.

"Wait, she still had another month to go at least, didn't she?" I asked, worried about Tammy and shocked that I hadn't heard the news yet. It was typical for gossip to spread like wildfire around here. I made a mental note to put together a cookie bouquet after I gave Steve a call to see what was up.

She shrugged her shoulders. "Not sure, just know she wasn't there today. Coach C was." The smile was back.

"Yeah? What's she like?"

"He, Mom. 'What's he like?'" she corrected me with a dreamy look in her eye, and it clicked. She had a crush on her teacher. This could not be happening to me. I wasn't ready for her to be noticing boys, let alone men.

"Oh?" I stalled, panic gripping at my chest. "Okay, what's he like, then?"

"Um . . ." She licked a dab of frosting from her finger, stalling as well. "He's got a great tan and these blue eyes that twinkle when he smiles. He is a little older, though." She had my attention now. There weren't any teachers at the school that fit that description, and Mr. Crouse, the history teacher I'd assumed she was first talking about who always covered in a pinch, without a doubt did not fit her description.

"Of course he's older; he's your teacher!" I rolled my eyes at her, and then I tried to proceed in a calm manner. "Does this coach have a last name?"

"Childress. But he told us to call him Coach C. Oh, and he let me be captain for basketball today!" she announced with glee, unconcerned that my face had pulled into a slight frown. Why did that name sound familiar?

"That's great, short stuff! Who won?" I called over my shoulder while going to get the edible gold dust from the pantry. It was a special touch I always added to the clover cookies.

"My team, of course," she answered with an exaggerated eye roll that made me shake my head in amusement before I turned back to the icing.

It wasn't until later that night, while on the verge of slumber, that it hit me. Rebecca Childress was a resident at Royal Hills. I'd managed to visit with her once or twice, but it wasn't normal for her to be in the day room when I was there. However, when we got together for Sunday dinner, Daddy always had amusing stories about the antics she had gotten up to that week. She had a thing for his asters. From what I could recall, I was pretty sure she'd had a stroke and could be forgetful. Sitting up and shaking off impending sleep, I racked my head for what he'd had to say about her in the recent weeks. All I could come up with was a passing mention that her husband had died due to complications from his lung cancer. Oh, and there was something about a son.

~oOo~

I'd been trying to hang curtains in my tiny, one-bedroom apartment to give it a homier feel when I banged my thumb with a hammer and ended up in the ER. Something about the fact that I couldn't bend it and that it was swollen to about three times its usual size convinced me to go in.

It was my lucky day.

It put me in the right place when Tammy Rose – Coach Rose to the kids – was brought into the ER in pre-mature labor. Crazy woman had been more concerned that her classes wouldn't be covered than she'd been about the life trying to crawl out from between her thighs. It was admirable seeing a teacher so worried about her charges; you didn't see that kind of dedication in big cities. Not that those teachers didn't care—it was just that here, it was more tight-knit, like family. And family looked out for one another.

"Coach Rose, can I offer my services?" I proposed, figuring why not, I was going stir crazy sitting around all day. Look how I'd ended up here. Ol' Mr. Harrison was doubtless getting sick of my offers to help him around the grounds, too. Every day, I'd stop and chat with him, getting the update for the day on Mom and lending a willing ear when he wanted to talk about his kid and granddaughter. I always ended the conversation with a: "Let me know if I can do anything around here." And as much as I loved my mother, checkers did become boring after a time.

Coach Rose hissed and sucked in a sharp breath. Letting it out with controlled timing, her eyes opened and focused on me. "Who are ya?"

"Trent Childress, Coach," I introduced myself with confidence.

"Rebecca and Michael's boy?"

I nodded. "One and the same, come back from Charlotte to look after Mom," I replied. Throwing in a wink for good measure, I added, "I was a middle school coach there, taught science on the side."

She turned a strange shade of purple and red, muttered some curse words, then barked at the man beside her, "I want him."

That was the end of it. They rolled her away and the man, who turned out to be Principal Stone, shook my hand and welcomed me aboard. He was very thankful that I was willing to jump in the next day.

In the weeks since, I'd had an amazing time. The staff was close-knit, yet welcomed me with open arms. There was no opening for a science teacher and no actual need for any cross-teaching in the small school, so I was able to make my sole focus coming up with fun ways to get the kids moving while teaching them the basics on a variety of sports. The kids were great also and very welcoming, little Candy Harrison in particular. She had a vibrancy about her that had endeared her to me on the first day of class. Her blue eyes always sparkled with curiosity and mischief, yet she had to be one of the most polite children I'd ever encountered. It didn't come from shyness, but from an inner maturity that I found remarkable in one so young.

When I discovered Lacey was her mother, it all made sense. The mother was extraordinary, so it followed that the daughter would be, too. I couldn't wait until Meet the Teacher Night so I could meet her mother—again. Of course, that wasn't going to be until a week after Easter. There would be a bake sale first. It was a fortunate coincidence I had a hankering for something sweet.

Chapter 3
~April~

Following St. Patty's Day, the orders started coming in strong and steady. That was typical this time of year, due to the large number of spring births in our area; I'd joked on more than one occasion about there being something in the water. Plus, there was planning for the Easter bake sale. I was staying late to double-check my inventory, along with getting pre-made dough blended and packed into the freezer to help speed the process as orders came due.

Before I knew it, my kitchen had been taken over once again. Now I was standing next to a table decorated with bunnies and eggs decorated in bright colors, peddling our wares. Candy had run off, saying she wanted to find someone that, "I had to meet." I was hoping she'd moved past the mysterious Coach C to someone closer to her own age.

"Enjoy, Steve," I said, thanking Coach Rose's husband for his purchase of two dozen honey carrot cookies. He stepped away, revealing my daughter, who had her hand latched onto the arm of my Valentine's Day egg disaster: Trent.

"Lacey," he murmured, his eyes meeting mine and igniting a tugging feeling inside of my stomach that crept lower the longer he looked at me.

"Hey, Trent," I choked a bit on his name. "Gonna support the school again?" His spreading grin changed the tug to a full on twist and pull, and I lost my breath.

"Least I can do, seeing how they employ me and all," he answered with a cheeky tone.

"Coach C?" I hazarded a guess, my nose scrunching up.

"Yes, ma'am. Nice to meet ya," he extended his hand. "Your daughter is a delight to have in class," he teased with a roll of his eyes. I laughed.

"I bet. I'm guessing you're aware of a certain crush?" I asked, leaning in so that gossipy ears could not overhear me, though our positioning itself was bound to start gossip.

He turned in towards me, his breath a warm whisper on my cheek as he replied, "Yes, I am, and I'm handling it by openly flirting with her mother."

I felt a snap inside of me and lost awareness of my surroundings for a moment. Had the man who had begun starring in my dreams just hit on me? I pulled back, shock on my face. His sexy smirk faded, replaced by a look of concern.

"Lacey, I'm sorry. Was that too forward of me?" He looked down and added a muttered, "Shit."

"I'm good, Trent. You just—you just surprised me is all," I consoled with a shrug of my shoulders and an offered grin. I hoped it didn't give anything away or make me look manic.

"Mom?" Candy interjected, and we looked down to her stricken face. Terrific.

"Candace, you dragged him over but failed to introduce us. However, as this is the kind gentleman who smashed five dozen eggs into me as a Valentine's gesture, I happen to already know who he is." She opened her mouth then shut it. Smart girl.

"Give me a dozen of each," Trent butted in, trying to ease the tension rising between her and me.

My head snapped over to him. "What are you going to do with that many calorie-laden treats?"

He threw his head back and laughed. "Why, Lacey, are you worried about my figure?" He gasped with a dramatic flair. "Have you been checking me out?" he teased further.

On impulse, I reached out and gave his arm a playful slap, my palm lingering on the firmness beneath.

His eyes dropped down to my hand, then flickered back up to my face. "Have dinner with me, Lacey. Please?"

My head nodded "yes" while inside, my mind was screaming warnings and a plethora of synonyms for "idiot" at me. Lacey Harrison didn't date. Everyone knew this; they'd learned and stopped asking. That was why his offer caught me so off guard—I was no longer used to it.

But how long did I plan to stay alone? Forever?

His face morphed into a glowing image of laugh lines and twinkling eyes, just like Candy had described to me a month ago. "Tonight, after you're done here?"

"Oh, I don't know. It's been a crazy couple of weeks and I'm about dead on my feet . . ."

"Trust me, I'll make sure you get to relax," Trent pressed, and against my better judgment, I agreed.

~oOo~

She agreed! I couldn't believe my luck. I knew the reputation she had for turning down men. I didn't know her story, but seeing how she had a kid, I could hazard a guess that she'd been skipped out on by the dad. That was the guy's loss, because Candy was a great kid, and her mother—her mother was something else. By some divine intervention, I was going to get a chance with her.

Now, I just had to figure out what in the Sam Hill I was going to do for our relaxing dinner date. There were times when my inability to think things through before speaking was rather annoying. To buy myself some time and to distract her, I reminded her of the cookies I'd requested.

"Royal Hills."

"I'm sorry?" Lacey asked.

"That's what I do with the cookies. My mom is a resident out there, and they are big fans of yours," I explained with a jovial laugh. The apples of her cheeks reddened then faded back to cream, a whisper of a blush that I couldn't be sure I'd seen but that sped my pulse.

I had to fight the sudden urge to kiss her. Paying Lacey for the treats, I told her I'd be back at the end of the sale to pick her up. Candy helped me carry the boxes to my car and then climbed in.

"What are you doing, missy?"

"Figured since you're heading to the same place as me, you could give me a ride, and we could have ourselves a little chat," she responded.

"Why are you going to the retirement home?" I asked, smiling at her tenacity.

"To help Grandpa with the tulips. We're planting the bulbs today," she replied with a broad smile. I thought about it, and it all came together. The groundskeeper was Candy's grandpa, and Lacey was the daughter he always spoke of with such fondness. Maybe he would be able to help me figure out what to do with her. I didn't want to drive off with Candy without clearing it with Lacey myself, so I jogged back over and found her in a debate over extract flavorings with Ms. York, who ran the school cafeteria.

Being as polite as possible, I interrupted to fill Lacey in. She patted my hand, giving it a squeeze that told me she enjoyed touching me, and gave me the okay followed with a mouthed "thank you." My step felt lighter going back to the car. That lasted until we were on our way and Candy turned to me, her arms crossed over her chest. *Oh, yes—our chat.*

"What are your intentions towards my mother?" she asked with sincere concern, and I had to fight a smile at how cute she was. She'd also surprised me by going in a different direction from what I'd expected: playing the protector instead of berating me for breaking her heart. Not that I was complaining. Getting the protective daughter talk would be much easier to deal with, I thought.

"So here's the deal," she began. "Mom doesn't date. Haven't figured that one out myself, but hey, it is what it is. In fact, until two months ago – when she met you – she never seemed to even notice men."

We'd just come to a stop at a red light, and I looked over at her. "Candy?" I hedged, unsure all of a sudden if the child I was sitting next to was as young as I'd thought, or a teenager.

She barked out a laugh. "Oh, come on, Coach C," she chirped, exaggerating her words as teen-aged, and apparently pre-teen, kids were known to do. "It's not a big town. Newcomers are rare. Who else could she have bumped into? It wasn't that hard to figure it out." She rolled her eyes, and I responded with a half-laugh. I wondered if Lacey realized how scary-smart her kid was.

"What was tricky, though, was figuring out how to get you two together."

This time I laughed full and loud. "Females are dangerous."

She grinned and winked at me. "You have no idea, Coach, no idea." We drove further down the road before she added, "Anyways, I'm pretty sure Mom's got the hots for you. If the way you were looking at her back there was anything to go by, you feel the same?"

I nodded. This had to rank in the top five weirdest conversations I'd ever had.

"I like ya, so I'm willing to help you out here. But if you hurt my mom, there will be consequences," she growled at me, and I felt a shiver run up my arms.

"Candace Harrison," I addressed her with formality to convey my sincerity, "I assure you, I don't enter relationships lightly; haven't been in one in quite some time, in fact. With your mom, I see much more than just a pretty face, and I feel honored that she is giving me the opportunity to get to know her more. That's all I can ask for right now: a chance – and time – to prove myself."

With pursed lips she assessed me. When she saw whatever she'd been looking for, she nodded.

"Alright then, glad we covered that."

The afternoon passed in a blur while I got dirt so far up under my fingernails I wasn't sure they would ever come clean. Shane – he'd insisted I call him by his given name as soon as Candy told him about my date with Lacey – had put me to work right alongside them. Also like Candy, he'd felt a friendly chat was in order while we planted tulips, the afternoon waning as we worked.

By the time we returned the gardening tools to the shed, the sun had moved across the sky and was beginning to set, the horizon bursting into a visual medley of purples, oranges, and pinks.

"Poetry," Shane said, breaking the amiable silence in which we'd worked for the last half hour.

"I'm sorry?"

"She likes poetry. Or, well . . . she used to . . . Lacey, that is," Shane fumbled, trying to give me dating tips, I thought.

"That so?"

"It is. She liked swinging on that old porch swing out back, too."

"I'll keep that in mind."

"You do that," he threw in, giving himself the last word.

An hour later, my first date with Lacey Harrison was underway. We were on a wide, rickety porch swing with a gaudy, floral-print cushion. I'd scrounged up an old quilt, tossing it over the back in case she got chilled once the sun had set and the night air settled in. A loaded picnic basket rested on the ground, complete with an iced-down jug of sweet tea. We started our date sitting up and eating off our plates with a properness that didn't fit either one of us. We ended up with her head in my lap and the quilt over hers, while I fed her bites and read from a poetry book I'd located in my mom's room.

Candy popped in and out, as did Shane, conveniently needing some thing or another from the porch, but for the most part, we were left alone. The evening was peaceful and relaxing, like I'd promised her it would be. I think having her family's approval went a long way toward her reaching that state; if they trusted me, so could she.

After she fell asleep in my lap, Shane helped me get her up and settled into his guest room, where Candy was already tucked in and snoring. Together, we laid her atop the quilts, and then I removed her sandals with care. I ignored Shane's chuckles while I kissed her toes.

Walking past him on the way out of the room, he whispered to me, "Doesn't count when she's not awake to remember it, son."

Chapter 4
~May~

"Oh, my God, Coach! How much salt did you put in these?" Candy cried out in disgust, spitting the salt-laden bite of cookie out of her mouth.

"Ummm . . ." I looked around for the measuring thingy I'd used, found it, and held it up. "I think it was this."

Her eyes bulged. "You put a quarter cup of salt into our dough?"

"I warned you I couldn't tell my left foot from my right in a kitchen. You're the baker's kid; I don't know why you needed me," I huffed and moved to the fridge. I was in desperate need of milk to rinse the salt from my mouth, considering I'd taken a bite of my own cookie at the same time she had.

"Because we are making our moms' chocolate-dipped shortbreads. Well, we're trying to, anyways," she tacked on and leaned against the counter with a defeated look that made me feel guilty. Lacey had been asked to do a guest lecture on being a small business owner at Wofford College in Spartanburg, the next town over. It had worked out perfectly for me to cover Sugar & Spice for her after school with Candy's help, giving us an excuse to be in the kitchen to make some Mother's Day treats.

"Hey," I chided, tugging her long, black pigtail, "don't give up. We've got time to try again. I'll even let you measure the salt this time," I offered, which earned me a giggle and a buck-toothed grin. We cleaned up the first round's mess and pulled everything out to start again. On the second pass, we measured everything out first, with Candace verifying my measurements as we went, before we started mixing anything. When we were done, we had a tempting platter of shortbread, which had been half-dipped in dark chocolate. Turned out we made a good team.

The weeks since Easter had been amazing. Each day, Lacey would make sandwiches on her fresh-baked bread and bring them over to the school so we could share lunch. We'd gone to a ball game, taken moonlit walks, and endured Chuck E. Cheese for Candy. We were comfortable holding hands now, yet I'd not had the nerve to try for a kiss. A few times I was pretty sure I'd seen the same longing in her eyes that I felt inside, but it just hadn't felt right — until now.

A lot was riding on those shortbreads. With their help, I was hoping I'd be able to woo my first kiss from her after dinner on Mother's Day.

~oOo~

The guest lecture had been nerve-wracking, yet invigorating. To me, the invitation had spoken of my success. I was doing well and it was reflected in my life around me. Candace was flourishing, growing like a weed, and acing her classes. Our relationship had never been more solid, our small blip a fading memory. Business was steady with Sugar and Spice. And then there was Trent. He'd been nothing but a gentleman with me, letting me set the pace so I could get comfortable with the idea of having a male in my life again and giving me the space I needed to be comfortable with him.

The best thing was that Daddy and Candy seemed to like him, as well. My guard dogs had let him in; it seemed nothing but fair for me to do the same. He wasn't going anywhere anytime soon, so I had no reason to fear abandonment again. Coach Rose had made the decision to stay home with the baby since the early delivery had resulted in some minor complications, and Trent had been offered and accepted her position. He was great with the kids at school, but there was an extra spark when he was with Candy, almost like she'd already earned a spot in his heart in a daughter-like way. I had to wonder if I was earning a spot there as well.

"Mom, let's go!" Candace shouted at me down the hall. "I have to help Gramps and Trent. They'll burn the home down if they try to work in the kitchen alone."

It was hard not to laugh at her obvious frustration and her grasp of the situation.

"I'm coming; just getting my shoes." After slipping my heels on, giving myself a light spritz of Guess perfume, and checking my hair a final time, I made my way to the front door, where I could hear her impatient footsteps before she came into view.

She stopped. "You look beautiful, Mom," she complimented with so much awe in her voice that I blushed.

I'd never had any reason to dress up, so she hadn't seen me go to the nines. Not that a coating of makeup and a soft cotton sundress was going all-out; it was just so much more than my usual jeans, tee, and slick of lip gloss.

I walked up and gave her a hug, then gave her pigtails a playful yank. "Thanks, short stuff. You look very nice as well," I replied, taking in her lace-trimmed Capri and tank set. "Shall we?" She nodded and we were off.

When we got to Royal Hills, Candy headed straight for the kitchen, and I went to the day room, where I made my rounds and visited with the residents. It was late enough that they'd already been served their evening meal, so the heavily-frosted pink and purple cupcakes I'd brought with me were well-received. Not all the residents had family close by to come celebrate the holidays with them, and I hated to see a mother or father forgotten.

I was visiting with Trent's mom when he came to fetch me.

"You are so lovely, dear. You know, I have a son—fine looking young man. Someday he'll come to visit me, and I'll have to introduce you two. You'd make a fine couple, and your babies would be adorable!" Rebecca gushed while patting my knee. I looked over her shoulder at Trent's soft sigh, and the anguish in his face broke my heart. Talk about bittersweet. It was clear that she approved of me for her son, but it was killing him that she couldn't remember him in the present, only as a thing of the past.

I gave him a slight nod, letting him know I would handle it, and he began to retreat to the dining room. Gesturing to the overflowing vase of colorful Gerbera daisies on the table next to her, I asked, "Are those from him? They're quite vibrant and indicative of his love for you."

She glanced over with a smile, "Yes! They were delivered . . ." Her voice trailed off and her brow furrowed. "Was . . . was Trent here earlier? Did he bring me the flowers?"

I looked up to where Trent had halted mid-step.

He pivoted back toward us, a firm smile fixed on his face, and came forward. "Hey, Mom. Do you remember our visit this afternoon?"

"Trent!" She came alive at the sight of him. "Trent, I was just telling Lacey about you. Come here and meet her. I want you to make me lots of grandbabies with her!"

I laughed. Trent was adorable when he blushed.

"Geez, Mom. Way to throw me under the bus," he teased, shooting me a wink as he leaned his tall form over her and gave her a gentle squeeze and a kiss to the forehead. Straightening back up, he came to me, extending his hand. I took it, and he raised my hand to his lips, brushing a kiss over my knuckles. "It's a pleasure to meet you, Ms. Lacey," he charmed.

Rebecca clapped and giggled next to us, and I rolled my eyes.

"See, I knew you two would be perfect! Now go on, Trent. Be a gentleman and take this young lady to dinner," she commanded, and I had a feeling I was getting a glimpse of the strong woman she used to be.

"You heard my mother; would you care to join me for dinner?"

"Hmm," I stalled, tilting my head to the side and placing a finger on my chin. "Sure, why not?"

Sugar & Spice

Trent helped me up before giving his mom a final hug and murmuring, "Happy Mother's Day" in her ear. He then escorted me to the table, which was set for five.

Dinner was delicious: barbeque meatloaf and garlic-cheese mashed potatoes, with a side of garden peas. I soon understood why there was an extra setting and why my father had been so willing to participate in the cooking. Daddy had met someone, right under my nose. At my shock, he'd laughed and told me it was no wonder I hadn't noticed, as enamored with Trent as I'd been.

While we ate, I did take notice, however. Cheryl would lean over, unashamed when she used her thumb to wipe food from the corner of my father's mouth. Likewise, there was no awkwardness when he slung his arm over the back of her chair and let his fingers tease over Cheryl's shoulders. Their actions showed a relationship beyond friendship had blossomed between them. *Where had I been?*

Dinner finished with Trent and Candy's amazing shortbread; it was the one sweet I did like. I'll admit that my eyes teared up a bit when they brought it out, and then we'd all had a good howl when Candy shared that they'd had to throw out the first batch and why. Dad and his new girlfriend took Candace across the yard to his house, leaving Trent and me to clean up the dishes.

I washed and Trent dried while we visited. He seemed to enjoy hearing about my lecture and some of the great questions the kids had asked, and then I laughed at myself for thinking of them as "kids" when they were just a few years younger than me. He gave me more details on the "salt incident," and I ended up laughing even harder, my hands slapping down in the soapy water and bubbles splashing up onto my top. I squealed in surprise, and then time stopped.

Trent leaned in, stopping when his mouth hovered just above mine. "Lacey, tell me it's okay to do this," he whispered, his sapphire eyes pleading with me. My eyes closed, my chin lifted a bit, and I puckered my lips.

And then we kissed. Slow and testing when our lips met, it built up as we gained confidence with each other, until we had to pull apart or risk suffocation. Both of us were left staring in awe at the other.

First his mom and then my dad had pushed us, encouraging us to take the chance we were being given.

Were we moving slower than we needed to be? Was my attraction to him more than fleeting? Could I trust him? All signs pointed to yes. He'd given me three months and a heart-stopping kiss. I could give him something in return.

    I was ready to give a little more.

Chapter 5
~June~

Summer was upon us, as was Father's Day, and for the first time in years I felt at odds. Candace and I had always made a production out of spoiling Daddy this time of year since his birthday always fell within a day or two of Father's Day. But we wouldn't be spoiling him this year. Cheryl had stopped by to see me at the shop; she wanted to take him to Myrtle Beach, which just happened to have Little River Casino not too far away. Daddy had always wanted to try a weekend of gambling but had never had anyone to go with him. She'd finished her sales pitch with: "So, do you mind if I take him away for the weekend?"

In my head, I'd screamed: "Of course I mind," but on the outside, I'd smiled and told her it was no problem at all and wished them a good time. I had to be happy that after all these years he had found someone that could make him smile, besides me. He had never dated after Mom, making me his sole priority. My father was moving on at last, learning to look after his own needs now that he did not have to worry about me all the time. Perhaps it was time for me to do the same: move on, take chances.

I'd become such a creature of habit and routine, living by the holidays because of the peaks and valleys in the baking business, that to have this weekend free all of a sudden – with the exception of some extra stock on the shelves – left me fidgety and antsy.

"We could do something for Trent," Candy suggested while helping me with a batch of cupcakes. They were our biggest seller on Father's Day weekend: red velvet cake with cream cheese frosting. I decorated them by piping on black icing to make them look like tuxedo shirts.

"For what?"

"Father's Day. Ya know, so you can chill out," she said with a laugh, exaggerating the chill out part. Her reaction was her subtle way to let me know that I was radiating my anxiety.

I thought about it. *Would it be a good idea, or would it backfire?* "I don't know, Candy. This will be his first Father's Day without his dad. It might be painful for him."

"That's just it, Mom. We need to help him with new memories. We can't just leave him to wallow in misery." For a nine-year-old, sometimes her perception of life in general left me amazed, though I was getting used to it. "Besides, I was kinda hoping . . ." she trailed off.

I stopped folding the batter and turned to her.

"Hoping what, short stuff?"

She was fussing with her fingers, then picking at a thread on her sleeve, her eyes fixed on the floor while she mumbled something that I couldn't make out, other than maybe the word 'dad.'

"Need you to say that again; I didn't understand a word of it," I teased her, offering her the stir spoon to lick.

She shook her head, declining the treat, and hopped up on the counter, locking her hands over the edge to support the movement.

"Um, I said I was kinda hoping maybe, one day, um, Trent could be my dad?"

My heart stuttered at her words. All these years, I'd convinced myself that Daddy could be enough of a male presence in her life, but it was now hitting me that

I wasn't protecting her by being a loner and depending on my father to be her sole male figurehead. All I had accomplished was to over-shelter her. Our life wasn't normal. All her friends had moms and dads to dote over them, show them examples of affection. She wasn't getting to witness that kind of love, and I worried that she would follow me down the hermit path.

I assumed my silence was making her nervous. Her eyes flickered up, then down, then back up to mine. I looked at my daughter – her features, the angles of her face – and with a shock, realized I could see Trent in them. She could pass for his if he wanted her—wanted us. Granted, I could have misread his intentions, but I didn't think I had. He'd gotten nothing more out of me than a handful of toe-curling kisses, and he was still here, still willing to court me at my own speed.

What am I doing? Taking a chance.

I exhaled, my teeth clenching as I blew the air through my lips. "What are we cooking?"

"Really?" she asked, her eyes shining with hope as her lips curled up into her beautiful smile.

"Really, really," I said with a stunted laugh.

She lunged into my arms, and it was my turn to smile. Yes, she was going to grow up. Yes, she would leave someday. But for right now, she was still my little girl, and seeing her happy was the most important thing in my world. I just hoped her happiness and my heart would not end up as collateral damage should this budding relationship take an abrupt turn and blow up in both our faces.

~oOo~

"What is all this?" I asked upon being led into the dining room by Candy. Lacey had called, asking me if I'd join them for dinner today. Never one to turn down home cooking, I'd accepted, assuming the dinner was in Shane's honor. However, I hadn't been expecting the spread that was laid out. I looked around to see where the rest of the guests were to help put a dent in the feast.

"Dinner," Lacey replied with a hint of sarcasm as she came out of the kitchen with a stack of plates. I rushed to take them from her, stealing a quick peck from her lips as I did. "I know it's a bit much, but

Candy and I figured that while the three of us would be the only ones here to eat the food, there would be others here with us in spirit," she explained in a gentle tone. I grasped what they had done, and their gesture touched my heart.

I took a moment to distribute the plates on the table before moving to take Lacey in my arms for a proper hello. Our kiss was just beginning to get a little heated when Candy giggled and we pulled apart. I turned towards Candy and opened my arms. "Do you have a hug for me, too?"

She nodded and ran over, her slight frame easily engulfed by my large one. Giving her a quick squeeze, I let my fingers tickle her sides until her relentless giggles left her gasping for breath.

"Stop! Please stop!" she begged, and I tickled harder. Shifting my eyes upward, I found Lacey watching us with a quizzical expression. It became one of shock as Candy's pleas became more desperate, and she uttered a breathless, "No more, Dad! I can't take it!"

I pulled my hands back immediately, feeling as if I'd just been punched; the air left my lungs in a whoosh.

"Candace Michelle!" Lacey gasped, and Candy ran from the room, mumbling her apologies. I wasn't sure what had just happened, but I wasn't angry. "Why don't you go ahead and have a seat, and I'll go talk to her?" Lacey suggested.

"Lacey," I began, "Don't be upset with her. I'm not." I did not want Candace – or Lacey for that matter – to feel awkward over the slip.

"Oh, Trent," Lacey sighed.

"I mean it, Lacey. That little girl has won a spot in my heart. This may be a little premature, but I'm going to put it out there and hope it doesn't scare you." Her eyes were wide while she listened, and my own palms were sweating profusely. "She's not the only one. You've got a spot there, too. Now, I'm not suggesting we run out and get married tomorrow, but Lacey, I wouldn't object to that being our future."

Our future. Not hers or mine, but ours. It sounded just about perfect to me.

"I'm falling in love with you," I added, just in case that point was not clear.

Lacey stood there speechless, her eyes shifting between me and the hallway that Candy had run down.

I wanted to hear her say it back, but I didn't expect it. In the last month, since our first kiss, she had begun opening up to me as much as I had with her, so I knew how afraid she was of committing herself. When she'd told me about Candy's dad Mark, I had run the gamut of emotions, experiencing everything from fury to jealousy over the situation. I had even gone so far as to do some research on one Mark Reynolds in an attempt to understand why he had been willing to walk away from them without a care.

His trail ran cold quick. He hadn't even graduated from the school that had offered up his scholarship. I was unable to find out the specifics; just that he'd been kicked out. What he was doing with his life was anybody's guess, but it was certain he was not a famous football player now. In the end, I'd decided that all that mattered was that Shane had the common sense to have Mark sign over all parental rights.

"I —" she started, and I held my breath, "I think I am too."

My heart began pounding and I smiled so big that my cheeks hurt.

Chapter 6
~July~

"You want me to touch a worm?" I asked, my squeamishness obvious to any observer. Candy, Trent, and even Daddy and Cheryl had ganged up on me and convinced me to take something called a "vacation." My worries over the shop were squelched when Cheryl offered to cover it for the weekend. I only had to bake what I could, and if she ran out, she was going to put up a Gone Fishin' sign. Everyone had found this hilarious but me — at first. Now that I was seated in the middle of a boat, trapped in the center of High Rock Lake, I could appreciate the joke.

"Geez, Mom, it's just a worm. Here." Sticking her hand out for the hook, Candy gave me an exasperated shake of her head. In her other hand was a squirmy, thick, brownish-pink thing. I think they'd called them night-wigglers or something like that.

"If you can't touch them, you might want to turn . . ." Trent tried to warn me as the hook pierced the worm with a wet squishing sound.

I gagged when I saw the juice ooze out of it, much to their amusement.

"I think I'll leave the fishing to you two. I'm going to read," I declared, pulling out the library book I'd borrowed for the trip and getting comfortable on the deck chair.

"Suit yourself, cupcake. You don't know what you're missing, though," Trent laughed. He bent over to kiss me, and I let him before pushing him off and groaning at the nickname he'd taken to using with me. Trent thought it was appropriate given my profession, and while I pretended to be unaffected by it, every time he used it, inside I squealed.

"Oh, I think I've seen enough to know I'm not missing anything, but you go on and have fun. And don't expect me to clean anything you catch, either. I work with eggs and flour, not scales and slime!"

The afternoon continued, and I had to admit it was peaceful. The soft rocking of the boat, the distant call of the loons and grebes in their nests around the shore, the warm breeze — it all worked together to lull me to sleep. It was unfortunate that I hadn't counted on dozing off. It was clear when Trent woke me with a very concerned look on his face that I had gotten way more sun than I should have.

"I think it's time for us to head back to the cabin, sleeping beauty," he joked.

I stretched, and the book fell from the chair. With an instinctive jerk, my hand darted out to catch it, and the skin on my arms felt like it was ripping from my bones. I looked over myself. Not only were my arms bright pink, the backs of my legs were too, and from the feel of it, so were my shoulders and back. I groaned while I twisted in an attempt to assess the damage. "A little help?" I asked, and Trent's hands took mine, freeing me from the lounge chair. "I'm cooked," I whined, and he chuckled.

"Sorry, I should have kept a closer eye on you, but Candy and I ended up catching enough stripers for dinner." He held up the storage bucket filled with lake water and fish, and I grimaced. "Then we decided to swim, so we've been overboard for the last hour. Do you know your daughter is a fish?"

Before I could reply, Candy appeared from behind him, shaking her head and spraying cold water all over me. Instead of feeling refreshing, the cold droplets felt like ice picks pelting my skin, and I whimpered aloud.

"Wow, Mom, that looks painful."

"It feels painful, too. I hope you have some aloe at the cabin." I turned my attention back to Trent. He had brought us up to High Rock, where he had a family cabin, and it was beautiful. The North Carolina mountains were so lush and green, even more so than upstate South Carolina. You couldn't help but imagine fairies and wood sprites hiding in the foliage; but fairy magic wasn't going to relieve this burn — aloe was.

"No worries, Lacey. Aloe, apple cider vinegar, manufactured sunburn creams; it's all there. Trust me; there's been no shortage of red noses on these trips. Let's get you back and into a cool shower so I can rub you down." It was a good thing I was already bright red, otherwise the direction my mind went with his words would have been apparent. He cleared his throat and shifted away from me. Maybe it wasn't just me who had gone there.

I hadn't missed sex per se, my limited experience with it not being anything memorable, but it was getting more difficult to spend so much time with Trent without thinking about our relationship moving to that next level.

Ignoring the way my pulse fluttered or how a smile was always pulling at my lips when I was with him wasn't an option. Not to mention the dreams. Oh, the dreams. Waking with a sheen of sweat and an ache needing to be quelled, yet not having the wherewithal to do anything about it, was maddening, to say the least.

Ever the perpetual worry wart, at the top of my list was whether or not we would be compatible when we did become intimate. Surely a male specimen such as Trent had plenty of experience under his belt. Would I look like a fumbling virgin, unsure of how to handle the movements of her own body?

My father's sage advice tumbled into my mind: You can only take one day at a time, and it's best to make that day count. With that thought, I settled into my seat with timid movements while Trent started up the boat to take us back.

~oOo~

Sugar & Spice

I felt like a right idiot. Within moments of climbing back onto the boat, I realized my plan to sneak up on Lacey wasn't a good one. She was burned—bad. I hadn't thought to make sure she'd applied sunscreen before she stretched out.

Having set Candy the task of starting dinner, I was now pacing in Lacey's bedroom. The sunburn ailment basket sat on her bed. I couldn't decide if I should stay in here to meet her, or if I should wait outside the door so she could dress first. Since she'd been in a bikini top and barely-there denim shorts, a lot of skin needed treatment, therefore getting dressed would have to wait. So I paced.

"Hey." Her voice, a soft whisper, caught my attention. I looked up to find her clad in a fluffy green towel that highlighted her eyes, and I felt the first stirrings of trouble. I was going to need to stay focused, be professional in my touch, and get out.

"Hey, yourself. Did the cool water help?"

"After a bit of adjustment on the shower head—at first it felt like razors. Oh, and I took some Tylenol as well." She laughed. "So, should I just lay on the bed, then?"

"That'd be great. I'll just turn around." I twisted as she moved past me, her clean scent settling on my tongue and in my nose. *Focus*, I chastised myself. I heard the soft rustle of fabric and the tiniest of squeaks from the mattress, and I could imagine her on her knees, crawling to the center . . . *professional, Trent.* I shook my head and squeezed my hands closed, then spread my fingers wide, stretching them.

"I'm ready."

Turning, my breath caught at the sight before me. Her silky, short, black hair feathered against her cheeks, and her forehead rested on her folded hands. Angry, red skin stood stark against the pale blue bedspread, until I reached the lower section of her back. Her pale bottom curved up from the bed in a soft sway, like a swirl of cream against the blue before becoming fiery-red again where the swell of her cheeks met the back of her thighs. Pulling my eyes from the shadowy space where her thighs met, I found the towel she'd cast aside on the floor. *Damn, now I was ready too.*

Only the proper upbringing I'd had kept me from ravaging Lacey; that, and sheer will power. I managed to behave like a gentleman while I smoothed the aloe-infused, orange-scented lotion onto her body. Her skin felt cashmere-soft beneath my fingertips, and I handled her with the care she deserved. By the time she was saturated with the cool cream, her pain killers had kicked in, and she was asleep, a small bit of drool beginning to escape the corner of her mouth. I grabbed a tissue and wiped off her face. Then I retrieved the soft blanket from across the foot of the bed, unfolded it, and covered her up. I kissed her forehead and departed to take my shower and find some relief of my own.

Turned out it was a good thing it was summer vacation. Compliments of her sunburn throwing off her temperature gauge, Lacey ended up getting sick, making me feel even guiltier. I insisted on her letting me move into her spare room so that I could be there to take care of her. After much reluctance and learning that her cold had progressed to pneumonia, she agreed. It took me another week and the pressing reminder that she had a birthday party to plan for Candy to get her to go to the doctor and get some antibiotics.

Chapter 7
~August~

Having Trent around so much was spoiling me. I was sorry that I had resisted, though he had been nothing but understanding, again giving me room to a degree. He was a tough nut to crack with regards to my health. I knew he blamed himself for my being sick, and no matter what I said, I couldn't convince him to believe otherwise. The strength of his concern spoke volumes about his feelings for us.

The three of us had clicked. There was no weirdness or adjustment period when he moved in. It was just a natural fit—once we worked out a bathroom schedule. I'll admit that I fell a little harder for him at the tenderness he was using to take care of me and Candy: my baby girl, whose tenth birthday party was scheduled for the next day, Saturday the fifteenth.

Daddy, Cheryl, Trent, and I had all been working hard to pull off the mermaid party she wanted, thanks to her obsession with a show about a trio of Australian teens who were mermaids. Trent had even convinced

Principal Stone to let us borrow the school's carnival dunk tank for the occasion and had promised to be the first one to sit on the bench. I baked up a storm with Cheryl's help, and we ended up with a table laden with sea-related goodies like sugar cookie shells, peanut butter and jelly sushi rolls, and sea salt caramels.

All her girlfriends from school had come, along with a couple of boys, which put me on guard and had Trent laughing at me. I got back at him by being the first to dunk him. The look on his face when I stepped up and drew my arm back had been priceless. Constant dough kneading gave you more muscle than most realized. Once his laughter had been well-doused, the kids – and some of the adults – took turns sitting on the bench as a reprieve from the muggy, hot, Carolina afternoon.

I was pleased when everyone ooh'd and aah'd over the mermaid cake. Bloody thing had taken me two days to make and decorate. Part of the decorations I'd made had included ten candles with metallic tinting in the shape of scales, which I put in the mermaid's tail. When lit, the strategic placement of the candles gave her tail the appearance of movement. When the time came to blow out the candles, Candy, although looking a little worse for wear with her dirty knees and bits of flyaway hair that had escaped her braid, was glowing with the euphoria of the day. She closed her eyes, her lips moved as she whispered her wish, and then she blew sure and strong. No candle was left burning.

"Hey, kiddo. How ya doing?" Daddy asked as he came to sit on the porch swing with me. I'd moved there after the cake had been served to take a break. I was beat.

"The burn has healed for the most part. I'm still a little tired from getting sick, but I'm getting there."

He nodded.

"I can't believe she's already ten," I added after a few minutes of silence, looking across the yard to where Trent was pushing Candy in the old tree swing.

"You just wait; time will pick up speed now. Next thing you know, she'll be talking babies," he teased, and I snarled at him. This made him laugh, and he pulled me into a one-armed hug. Content, I settled my head on his shoulder. "She'd make a great big sister right now, though."

His comment lingered in the air. I couldn't think of how to respond to that because, as soon as he'd said it, I could picture it. Unlike when Trent's mom had mentioned it back in May, I now knew I loved him and would love to have a family with him. I could picture it, because it was now possible in my own mind.

Knowing he'd made his point, my father offered to keep Candy for the rest of the weekend so I could get some rest. I had been struggling to keep up, what with fighting pneumonia and all. In addition, the back-to-school bake sale was coming up, and there was clothes shopping and supply gathering for Candy to be done. A small break to recharge sounded wonderful, and I told him so. I thanked him with a hug and set off to find Candy to let her know what the plans were. Trent stood by as I talked to her and kissed her goodbye.

"Let me give you a ride home?" he offered.

I waved him off. "I can walk. You've got another hour of daylight. You should stay and enjoy yourself."

"Lacey, I'm thirty-eight years old, and I know it. I've enjoyed myself plenty for an old man. Now please, let me escort you home and share a relaxing glass of wine while I rub your feet."

"How can I refuse an offer like that?" I answered, and we made our way to the car, saying our farewells to the lingering guests along the way.

When we got to the house, I left him to open the wine for breathing and went to take a shower. Feeling more refreshed, I dressed in a pajama set consisting of shorts and a crop top, grabbed the yummy-smelling lotion he'd been using on my sunburn, and went to find him.

I found Trent on the screened-in back porch, watching the sky in the beginning stages of twilight, the pinks and oranges beginning to creep in from the edges. The futon couch had been opened into its bed form, and all the decorative pillows were stacked up against the wall in a pile. Despite the surrounding screen, he'd lit the citronella candles to ensure the mosquitoes stayed at bay and had docked his MP3 player in the base I kept out there. New age music cascaded from the mounted speakers, creating an atmosphere of serenity. White wine sat in an ice bucket to the side, while two filled glasses sat next to it. Trent lifted one and offered it to me. With a giggle, I took it and handed him the lotion, along with a set of puppy dog eyes.

One glass of wine turned into two while he rubbed my feet. Two glasses turned into three before he had me roll onto my stomach and sat atop my thighs so he could massage my back, working the knots out of my sore muscles. Loose and limber from a combination of exhaustion, the massage, and the wine, I sighed when his fingers trailed under the hem of my top, teasing along my sides until he brushed the sides of my breasts. I rolled into his touch, and when my eyes met the hunger in his, I sat up and reached for his mouth with my own. His hands continued to move over me, a strong need pulling us closer, and I gave in.

~oOo~

Morning came with a slight headache and a feeling of utter bliss that lasted until I moved, feeling the warm body beside me, and then it all came rushing back. Next to me, her hair tousled and the sheet molding to her tan – if somewhat flaky – skin, was a nude Lacey. Though she was exquisite to look at, my stomach sank at the realization that after months of tap dancing around the sexual tension building between us, we'd crossed that line while inebriated. My mother would not be proud.

I'd wanted our first time to be romantic and special. So many times, I'd envisioned how the evening would go once she was ready. Relaxing music in the background, candles casting a sensual glow over our flesh as we came together, a nice wine—I'd wanted it all. A soft sigh from Lacey drew my attention back to her. I studied her face, examining the tiny blue veins that crisscrossed the thin skin of her fluttering eyelids. She rolled over, her lips parting a bit, and the sheet caught before slipping down to reveal a single breast and the upper part of her abdomen. I knew if I continued looking, I would want to relive the pleasurable tumble we'd taken last night, and I was pretty sure we needed to sort things out before we did that again.

With reluctance, I pulled my eyes away and found myself looking round the porch. My gaze flitted from the extinguished citronella candles, to the dock, to the empty bottles of wine on the floor, and I smiled. Seemed last night had been perfect after all.

"Trent?"

I smiled down at her confused, sleepy face. "Morning, cupcake. How are ya feeling?"

She sat up, grabbing the sheet to cover herself. Her modesty was endearing after the night before. "It wasn't a dream, was it?" she asked, her words quiet and her eyes bright. I shook my head and moved my arms to surround her. She settled against my chest. "Was I okay? Do you have any regrets?" she murmured.

"What?" I laughed. "Of course you were, Lacey, and I have zero regrets. You know I love you, and you love me, so what we did is nothing to be ashamed of. It was a physical expression of our feelings, simple as that," I reassured her. "*You* don't have any regrets, do you?" I tacked on, now feeling uncertain.

"No, not at all. It was time. Past time," she laughed and tilted her head for me to catch her mouth in a tender kiss. "If my first time had been like this, I doubt I could've waited so many years to do it again."

R.E. Hargrave

I knew she was joking, but her words were weighted with a sadness I wanted to replace. I vowed to myself that I would.

Chapter 8
~September~

September came at us with a fury that left little time for rest or reflection. I was thankful to have the back-to-school bake sale out of the way, where enough money was raised to ensure that the art department had ample funds for their annual supply budget. After that, we tackled the next obstacle—getting ready for school.

Trent was in a slight panic. While cross-course teaching wasn't normal in the small school, the gym teacher was expected to handle the one-month section of Health that gave the fifth graders their first taste of sex education. He wasn't panicking due to the course itself, since he'd taught it before. It was because Candy would be one of his fifth graders, and the whole town knew we were a couple now. Not that an opportunity to be intimate again had presented itself in the end of summer madness, but at least we still had our stolen kisses and moonlit walks. Our walks often included Candy.

The last two weeks had proven my earlier claim: years of waiting to be intimate again would have been impossible if the longing I now felt to have Trent in my bed again was anything to go by.

I had also come to the conclusion that a small part of my pneumonia lingered because of my sporadic sleep and less-than-ideal eating habits, which were the result of my being so busy. I hadn't gotten a chance to have a full recovery, and I was now paying for it as fatigue overtook me earlier each night, dragging me into bed and knocking me out before I'd even settled onto my pillow.

I didn't feel it was right for my boyfriend to teach my daughter about the birds and the bees beyond the extreme basics I'd already covered with her over the years. Therefore, I made the decision to expand on our usual back-to-school traditions by having "the talk" with her over a girl's weekend in Charlotte, complete with bra and pantyhose shopping. It was time to face facts; her tops were no longer sitting on a flat chest. She was my daughter without question, so I would not have been surprised if she were to begin her cycle sooner rather than later, too, which was another reason to go ahead and do this.

Labor Day weekend found us in a hotel with pre-packaged, preservative-laden junk food for our girl talk. I was surprised how awesome Double Stuf Oreos turned out to be, and I might have developed a slight addiction to white cheddar ChipIns: popcorn turned into chips. Our conversation started off with a bit of awkwardness, but once we got into our talk, I found she was more knowledgeable than I'd suspected. I did have to correct a couple of misconceptions she had, such as her belief that oral sex could result in pregnancy. Trent joked later that night on the phone that I should have let her hold onto that belief until she got married.

It was during our second day in Charlotte that Hurricane Madeline barreled down onto the Carolina coastlines. Had we not been out hitting all the stores and getting mani-pedi's, I might have paid closer attention to the weather reports and taken us back to Union earlier that day.

"Evenin' ladies. Successful afternoon, I see," the hotel desk clerk greeted us as we crossed the lobby, laden down with bags. I smiled, and Candy nodded with enthusiasm. She was excited about some of our purchases, an Edgar Allan Poe tee she'd found with a pair of hands holding a heart in particular. It was pretty weird but kinda cool. The fact that the shirt had piqued her curiosity and prompted her to ask if we could stop at a bookstore and get her a copy of *The Tell-Tale Heart* didn't hurt, either. "So, will you be heading out to beat the storm, or going ahead and staying on for tonight?"

"Do you mean Madeline? Last I heard, she was still churning way offshore."

"Yes, ma'am, and no, she gained energy and made landfall quicker than expected. Coastal towns have been evacuated, and upstate South Carolina has been put on alert," he explained.

"Oh, dear," I sighed, my thoughts going at once to Daddy and Trent. "Let me make a couple of calls, and I'll let you know for sure. For now, we'll plan on staying the night."

"Very good, ma'am."

Candy and I made our way to the room and dumped the bags in the corner. She headed to the shower, and I retrieved my cell phone, calling Trent.

"Cupcake!" he answered, and I barked out a laugh.

"Would you stop with that already?"

"Nope, you love it." I could hear his smile through the phone and my chest tightened. I missed him.

"Yeah, you're right, I do, but I love you more than the goofy name," I said in a soft timbre.

"I miss you, Lacey. And Candy. When are my girls coming back?"

"Well, that's why I was calling. I just found out about the warnings for the upstate. Do you think we should stay put until it blows over, or try to beat it and get home?"

"I'd love to have you home, but it's been raining steady all day and the wind is kicking up something fierce. I was just about to head out to Royal Hills; your dad called and asked if I'd help board up the windows."

"Oh, wow. Is it really that bad?" I asked, worried. Daddy hadn't had to board up the windows since Hugo, which had made landfall as a category four back in 1989.

"Afraid it is. Last report said it hit Myrtle Beach as a category five. I did the shop windows this morning and just finished your house," he admitted.

"Thanks for looking out for us, Trent. I guess we'll stay on and check in with you in the morning. School starts in two days, so we can't stay here forever."

"On that, Principal Stone already called me to let me know they've pushed it back a week. The town's expecting to have quite a mess to clean up." A loud crash sounded through the phone. "I should get going, cupcake."

"Okay. Are you going to stay out at the home after you do the windows?"

"Yep, I doubt it'll be safe to drive by the time we're done. Besides, Mom's never been good with storms, so I reckoned she might want me there regardless." He laughed, and I sniggered with him. Since we'd become an official item, Rebecca's short term memory had shown a miraculous improvement. According to Trent, it was just further proof that women, as a species, were calculating.

"Give Rebecca my love. Oh, and Trent?"

"Yes?"

Sugar & Spice

"Keep an eye on Daddy . . . his knees aren't what they used to be, and he really shouldn't be climbing ladders."

"I promise. G'night, Lacey. I love you."

"Love you, too. Night, Trent." I ended the call, a sense of foreboding creeping over my skin.

One night turned into three before the storm blew itself out and the road crews were able to get the highways open again. Bedraggled and weary, Candy and I pulled part way into our drive, avoiding the large tree limb that lay across a big portion of it.

"What happened to our house?" Candy asked, just as dumbfounded as me. A second branch had punched through a section of the roof; at least one window – that I could see – was smashed, despite having been boarded up; and Candy's old swing set, which should have been in the backyard, lay twisted in the front.

Knowing it couldn't be ignored, we got out of the car and waded through the debris in the yard. Mounting the porch steps, we found the front door standing open. A few inches of water remained; however, the mark of the high water line was clear several inches up the walls. I stood at the threshold, trying to wrap my head around the mess that stretched out before me. The only sounds were Candy's quiet whimpers while she stood beside me and reached for my hand. I was pulling her into a hug when a possum scampered from the depths of the house, running past us as if we weren't even there, and she yelled in surprise.

"Come on, back to the car. We'll deal with this later. Right now, we need to go find Trent and Gramps," I suggested, guiding her back to the vehicle. I didn't dare share with her that I was not looking forward to what might be waiting for us. If my house was this damaged in town where it was nestled in amongst other homes, it was safe to assume that Royal Hills, on the outskirts with nothing around to soften an onslaught, was much worse.

~oOo~

I was out back, setting a new window, when I heard the gravel crunching under an approaching car. My heart raced, and I hoped it was Lacey and Candace. Phones had gone down right after we'd spoken the night Madeline came on land, so I'd been unable to reach her to fill her in. I hadn't even been able to drive to her because of the road conditions. There was also the small fact that since it stopped raining, I had been working 'round the clock to patch up the holes in the home, acting in Shane's stead. I hadn't even had a chance to do a drive-by to see what Lacey's house or the store looked like. All my time had been spent here, with the exception of that first night.

"Trent!" Lacey's distraught voice cried. I set my tools down and headed round the porch. As soon as we spotted each other, she rushed to me. I stood still, opening my arms to her. She fell against my chest, mumbling about how much she'd missed me and how awful the damage to her house was. I stroked her hair, shushing her while I cringed at what I had to tell her. My stomach dropped when Candy piped up, asking where Shane was.

"He's over at Spartanburg Regional," I replied in a somber tone.

Lacey pulled back from me, her face scrunched with a lack of understanding. "Why? What happened? Did he fall from the ladder?" she asked, the worry on her face increasing with each question she asked.

"Lacey, Shane had a heart attack."

Chapter 9
~October~

    A month had passed since Trent had uttered the words that had turned my world upside down. At least he'd ripped the bandage off fast rather than starting with the small injuries and working his way up. Guiding me over to sit on the swing, he'd given me a few minutes to absorb his words before he summarized the extent of the damage. The heart attack had happened while Daddy was up on a ladder; it was soon after Trent had arrived, for which I was thankful. Otherwise, Daddy might have laid out in the storm all night. Instead, Trent heard his garbled yell when the attack hit and my father fell. He cracked a rib and broke a leg on his way down. And I'd been worried about his knees . . .

    While at the hospital getting the broken bones set, a second attack had hit him, resulting in emergency valve replacement surgery. My first reaction, born of a feeling of uselessness and utter shock at the situation, had been to get angry at Trent and Cheryl for not letting me know. Trent, of course, was able to calm me down enough to make me see sense. He pointed out that they'd tried, but it had been out of their hands, so they'd done what they could by focusing on getting my father's needs met.

We relocated to Daddy's house, which by some miracle had not been damaged, as an interim solution. The insurance adjusters were working as fast as they could but the town had incurred record amounts of damage and it was slow going. I had no idea when my house would be livable again, or even if it ever would be. Besides, Daddy's house was easier to use as a headquarters, considering it was just across the yard from the home, almost an outbuilding of the facility.

Trent proved to be a godsend where my daughter was concerned. I had closed Sugar & Spice until further notice, allowing me to be over in Spartanburg during the day, while Trent made sure Candy got to school, helped her with her homework, and even had dinner waiting when I'd drag back in late in the evening. The stress was grating on me. I was more tired than ever and was having trouble eating because my stomach felt off most of the time. I chalked it up to the bad hospital cafeteria java. I'd forgotten what sleep was.

Sugar & Spice

To my dismay, the PTA voted during the October meeting to go forward with the bake sale. They thought a little routine would help Union citizens to recover a feeling of normality as we headed into the chaos of the holiday season. The one difference in this year's sale, however, would be that in place of money, the folks would barter with man-hours and services. The PTA would then send the volunteers where they were needed, based on requests turned in to the help box.

Daddy was chomping at the bit to get out of the hospital and back home. He'd never been one to be idle, and being told he was going nowhere for at least eight weeks, maybe more, had made him miserable. We had to assure him that between the three of us – Trent, Cheryl, and me – Royal Hills was being looked after. He didn't buy it, though, until Trent brought his mom over to visit with Daddy. Rebecca was a spitfire that was for sure. The first thing she'd done had been to rib Daddy about his young fanny landing itself in the hospital before any of the old geezers out at the nursing home. They'd joked and laughed for the next hour, and Daddy thanked me when we left.

R.E. Hargrave

That had become the first of many "field trips" with various residents, sometimes two or three at a time. It gave them all something to look forward to, and we noticed a marked improvement in my father's attitude and recovery, enough that I was able to start spending less time at the hospital and more time focusing on Candy. We still had her costume to arrange, and of course, a bake-fest to endure.

Candy and I went round in circles over the costume, me wanting something cute and her wanting it to be more grown up now that she was in double digits. Once, the argument even reached the point of screaming and slamming doors. She was going to be a fantastic teenager. In the end, we compromised. She was going to be a scarecrow with the painted-on face, braided pigtails, and straw hat, but instead of overalls, she would wear a denim dress and heeled cowgirl boots.

Trent had somehow managed to find time to repair the shop, which had suffered minimal damage. So three days before Halloween, I unlocked the back door, and we all filed in: most of the moms, a couple of the teachers, Candy, and me. Two days later, we emerged with red eyes, stringy hair, and flour in every pore, but with the largest haul we'd ever managed. This was going to be the mother of all bake sales. It had been advertised in the paper and on the local radio station, but we were still surprised when people from out of town showed up Halloween morning, towing all manner of lumber, roofing shingles, and other supplies. The piles of brownies, cookies, bat-shaped chocolates, breads, and pies dwindled, to be replaced by the sounds of singing and hammering being carried on the wind.

We'd been passing out invitations for trick-or-treaters to come out to Royal Hills later that night. The school bus driver Ms. Jenny volunteered to play taxi for the night in exchange for an assortment of mini loaves. Late afternoon had crept over the town when the last of the goods were distributed amongst the workers. Tired but happy, Candy and I drove back to the house, where our costumes waited for us.

I got changed into my costume, a zombie baker, and was in the kitchen pouring the bags of candy into the large plastic cauldron we used for handing out the treats, when the doorbell rang with the first of the trick-or-treaters. Knowing

Candy was down the hall getting herself ready, I hurried to get the door, excited to see what creations the kids had come up with this year. My hand was inches from the doorknob when a small shriek from the bathroom made me turn and jog down the hall. "Candy? Everything okay, short stuff?" I called through the closed door.

"Mom?" Her voice sounded off, making me even more concerned.

"Yeah, baby, it's me. I'm coming in," I warned. Pushing the door ajar, I found Candy gaping at me in a state of shock and holding a wad of bloodied toilet paper.

"I think I got my period," she said in a strained whisper.

I was pulled into a vortex, the rest of her words becoming incoherent while my heartbeat pulsed in my head and the room spun.

"Period?" I choked out. My health symptoms over the last couple of months hit me like a wrecking ball: fatigue, nausea, aches. My period had always come like clockwork; with the first of the month around the corner, I should be about to start, but Candy's reminder had me counting.

My stomach crawled into my throat as I realized that with all the craziness we'd been dealt in September, I hadn't noticed I'd skipped. I hadn't had my period since the first of August . . . and two weeks later, I'd been with Trent. Had I done it again and gone two for two?

~oOo~

"You've gotta be kidding me," I heard Lacey mutter as I came around the corner to see why the door remained unanswered. I was met with the sight of her slumping to the ground in a faint outside the bathroom. With a worried, "Lacey!" I lunged forward. My motion was halted by Candy's soft, "Mom?"

Cautious, my eyes remained fixed on Lacey while I took another step closer, and I called out to her, "Candy? What happened, short stuff?"

"Don't! Don't come in here, Trent, please," she called back in a weak plea. "It's, um, girl stuff," she added, her voice almost too quiet for me to hear. But I did hear, and it was enough to make me blanch. This was so not my territory.

"Ung . . ." Lacey moaned, blinking while I watched her come out of her faint. I wanted to go to her, hold her in my arms, but with the door open, I wasn't stepping an inch forward. She looked into the bathroom and then over at me and paled. I couldn't believe she wasn't better prepared than me to handle this moment in Candy's life.

"Lacey, cupcake, is there anything I can do?" I offered, hoping for an excuse to back away.

Nodding her head, she gave me a disheartened smile. "Can you cover the front door for a bit while I sort this out?" she asked, just as the bell's shrill chime rang through the house again.

"On it!" I clapped my hands, spun on my heel, and hurried to open the door, cauldron of candy in hand. I'd make it up to Lacey later — maybe a foot rub before she got a chance to fall asleep on me again.

If she didn't relax soon, I was going to have to step in and slow her down. I didn't think she'd stopped going since Candy's birthday party two and a half months ago. The sad thing was, I'd been just as busy. Between looking out for Royal Hills, teaching, and stepping in as caretaker for Candy, I was every bit as tired as Lacey when we climbed into bed at night.

I didn't mind, though. It might have been tiring, but I'd never felt such fulfillment as I had over the last few months since I'd moved to this small town. I belonged here. I'd found happiness in Candy's smile, in Lacey's love, and in my mother's recognition.

Chapter 10
~November~

Two lines. I twisted the plastic stick around, moving the little window from the right side to the left. Still two lines. *Shit*. I groaned and dropped my head into my hands.

"Hurry up, Mom. I need to get in there," Candy yelled as she rapped on the bathroom door. Startled, I fumbled the test, and it fell to the floor, landing result side up and staring me in the face, mocking me.

"Just a sec." I finished washing my hands and gathered the trash from the kit, cramming all of it, test included, into the plastic shopping bag I'd snuck into the house, I stashed it all under the sink towards the back, plastered a smile on my face, and opened the door. "All yours, short stuff."

"Thanks," she answered, pushing past me and closing the door.

It had been an interesting week. With Candy's new development, I'd pushed my apparent problem to the backburner so I could be there for her. I'd expected she'd start early, but I was still surprised. Perhaps she had been more affected by the aftermath of the storm and Daddy's hospitalization than I'd realized.

After all the drama over her costume, she'd changed her mind about dressing up and going out, opting to stay in with me instead. Trent had offered to man the door, leaving us girls to bond in the living room. While nibbling on Halloween candy, we watched chick flicks like *Sisterhood of the Traveling Pants*. We'd ended up crashing during our last movie, waking up stiff the next morning with upset tummies from all the junk food.

Trent spent most of the weekend in town helping with the rebuilding. While he was gone, Candy and I worked in the nursing home's kitchen, preparing meals for the residents and fixing sack lunches for the volunteers. Cheryl was staying with Daddy, which made it possible for me to spend more time helping. My father was on track to come home in about two weeks, and everyone was already planning to make it a huge Thanksgiving Day dinner celebration.

R.E. Hargrave

A week had passed before I could think about my revelation, and another week to work up the nerve to go buy the test and get the confirmation I didn't need. I was having a hard time convincing myself that everything would be okay each time I tried to envision telling Trent, even though I knew he would think I'd done it on purpose to secure a father for Candace.

Another week passed as I ran through every possible scenario. Trent was acting suspicious, finding excuses to be away; or I was just being paranoid. Granted, it was understandable, since I had not been my normal self either; I'd been skittish whenever he went to give me a simple hug, appraising when we kissed, and flighty. But at least I knew why I was acting weird; I hadn't a clue where Trent was concerned. It was doing my head in. A conversation with Rebecca convinced me that it was time to tell him, for better or worse.

Without realizing it, I had been cradling my belly while looking out the window at nothing when Rebecca came in the dayroom. "Is he happy about the news?" she asked behind me. I'm not sure why, but I felt no need to be evasive or act like I didn't know what she was talking about.

"I don't know. I haven't told him," I responded with honesty, turning to face her.

"And why's that?"

"I'm scared," I admitted after a few moments.

"Of what, child?" She'd taken my hand and pulled me over to sit next to her on the sofa.

"That he'll leave me like Mark did."

"You know my son better than that, Lacey. Use your head, but listen to your heart, child." She patted my hand and took a deep breath. "Do you love him?"

"I do," I answered at once, feeling myself warm inside and out with the admission.

"He loves you, too. I'm his momma; I know. The rest will work itself out."

We sat in silence for a while, a weight lifting off my shoulders while the decision to tell him solidified in my heart.

"Okay, I'm ready to rest," Rebecca announced beside me. "Can you help me to my room for my afternoon nap, Lacey?"

I did as she asked, getting her settled on her bed and adjusting the blinds so she could watch her hummingbirds. "See ya for dinner, Rebecca. Thanks for the chat," I said, giving her a quick hug.

"Thank you, child, for taking care of my boy," she answered, hugging me back. For the first time, it dawned on me that I could have more. It had always been Daddy, Candy, and me—but wasn't there room to grow? Isn't that what families did? I shook my head with a soft laugh while I walked back downstairs. This family was already growing, whether anyone liked it or not.

~oOo~

As was typical, the month sped by, the students becoming more distracted the closer the holiday came, and it was only Thanksgiving. I knew next month would be even worse. It was this time of year that made me grateful that my job title ended at PE teacher. Trying to make a class full of kids focus on actual fact learning was next to impossible when they were so anxious to start their vacations.

Shane was doing better and would be home the next day. The week before, during our visit, he'd made a request of me when Lacey stepped out to use the bathroom. I was pleased that I'd been able to locate what he had in mind and had even found something I liked while I was searching. Even though I'd gotten some strange looks from Lacey when I'd come home late and couldn't explain where I'd been, I knew it would be worth it.

After much deliberation, I'd come to the conclusion that if I continued to wait for the right time to present itself, it never would. There would always be some new problem or bake sale or botched supply order or . . . or . . . or . . . The possibilities were endless. The old saying of: "Why put off for tomorrow, what you can do today?" wouldn't let me wait. In my mind, it boiled down to the simple fact that I loved Lacey, and I wanted her to be mine forever. Her and Candy.

Lacey's health had started improving, which gave me some relief. She was regaining some of the weight she'd lost during her months of illness and the subsequent stress over the house and her dad. I hadn't been able to figure out why she kept insisting on eating at the hospital cafeteria – since it kept making her sick – but I'd learned my lesson regarding her stubbornness back in July. So I was staying silent and just keeping an eye on her. I wouldn't hesitate to put my foot down and make her go see the doctor if she started looking too thin again. It helped that the decision had been made to forgo the Thanksgiving bake sale and just do a holiday sale mid-December. That meant one less thing she needed to worry about.

Candy had wanted to go to a friend's house for a sleepover, which gave Lacey and me an evening alone for the first time since August. We'd spent the day starting to get things ready for the following celebration. Cheryl had helped earlier in the day before she'd left to see Shane. When we called it quits, the pies were done, salads were made, rolls were set to rise overnight, and the turkey was dressed and ready to slide into the oven at the crack of dawn. At my offer, Lacey went up to shower while I stayed downstairs to clean up the mess. *Something I've been doing a lot of in recent months,* I thought to myself with amusement.

Making my way through the dark halls, I entered the bedroom I shared with Lacey to find her curled up in a ball on top of the comforter and sound asleep. I stood there and watched her for a while, thinking about how much this year had thrown at her and how she just kept getting back up. She was superwoman in the flesh. Covering her up and brushing her bangs away from her face, I kissed her forehead and whispered my love against her skin. Not wanting to risk waking her – she'd gotten so little rest of late – and knowing I wasn't sleeping anytime soon, I opted to take my thoughts out to the back porch. I was exhausted, but my brain was going too fast to sleep; I was nervous about what Shane and I had planned for the next day.

Ten minutes later found me settling onto our porch swing with a tumbler of cognac in my hand and my thoughts on high speed. I thought of everything, from how they would all react tomorrow, to how I was the last of the Childress line—for now. I was getting up there in years, and while Lacey was young, there was no guarantee that she wanted more children, with me or anyone else. Hell, we'd have to be a lot more intimate for that to even be a possibility. My chuckle broke the silence, laced with melancholy. Would things ever slow down enough for us to just be us?

The level in my glass gradually dropped while I deliberated. By the time the cognac was gone, a chill had settled in the air, and my joints were beginning to ache. I took my glass to the kitchen, locked up the house, and fumbled through the dark. A numb buzz overtaking me, I crawled into bed and wrapped myself around Lacey's resting form.

Without opening my eyes, I inhaled Lacey's scent on the pillow, making my morning situation a bit stickier. In my state of half delirium, I shifted over to pull her closer, hoping we might be able to take advantage of the holiday morning. I was met with cold sheets. My eyes blinked open to verify that I was alone, though the smells wafting up from downstairs should've been enough. She was already back in the kitchen. After a not-so-quick shower, I joined her, dressed in comfortable jeans and my Carolina Panthers sweatshirt.

Lacey wasn't alone. Candy and Cheryl, along with my mom and a couple of the other ladies from the home, were all sitting around, sipping their teas and coffees and nibbling on what looked to be fresh muffins. Lacey brought me my coffee, prepared just the way I liked it with just a splash of cream, and an orange-cranberry piece of heaven. I'd just begun to dive in when Shane appeared outside the large country kitchen. He started to approach me, his walker making his progress slow, so I gave Lacey a kiss, ruffled Candy's hair, and hugged my mom before meeting him halfway.

"How ya holding up, son?"

I shrugged. "Alright, I guess. Kinda nervous. How about you?" He'd been home for two days now, and they'd been busy ones.

"Can't complain. I wanted a chance to say thanks for running those errands for me. I want tonight to go perfect," he said, his eyes darting round to make sure we weren't being overheard.

"It was my pleasure. You've got great taste."

"Who has great taste?" Lacey asked, coming up behind me and threading her arm around my waist.

I leaned down to kiss her forehead. "Your dad does, of course."

She laughed like I'd hoped she would. "Morning, Daddy. Can I get you some tea or a bowl of fruit?" she asked Shane, moving to give him a tight squeeze.

Shane huffed. "I want my holiday joe, heavy on the Kahlua, and a plate of bacon and cheesy scrambled eggs," he said with a pout.

Cheryl had walked over and joined our small group by this point. "Shane Harrison, you will do no such thing!" she chastised him.

"Do you want to land yourself right back in that hospital?" Lacey added, ganging up on him right alongside Cheryl.

"I'd take the tea and fruit and hightail it out of Dodge, Shane," I laughed.

"Knew there was a reason I liked you, son. You're a smart one," he replied to a round of laughter. "Tea will be fine, thank you, kiddo."

Lacey went to get his tea, and I looked away while Shane and Cheryl shared a private good morning moment. Once he had his drink in hand, we left the ladies to their kitchen and went to turn on the Macy's parade and wait. Dinner would be served in about six hours, so we had about eight until our lives would change.

Chapter 11
~December~

Sitting around the table, listening to the light banter and the clatter of silverware on the china, I sipped my apple cider and felt happy. I knew when I'd woken up this morning snuggled in Trent's arms that I would tell him tonight, and we'd go from there. Having kept a close eye on him all day with his mom and Candy – all of them, really – I'd become convinced that, while he would be shocked, he would be pleased. Family meant too much to him for him not to be. It was with that assurance that I was able to relax and enjoy the huge meal.

"If I can have everyone's attention?" Daddy spoke up, his voice rising above the chatter and drawing everyone's eye. He looked nervous, which made me wonder what was going on. Daddy was always cool and collected. I looked to Cheryl, and she looked as confused as I felt. So I moved on, my eyes landing on Trent, who seemed rather fidgety as he stood up also, turning to me when Daddy turned to Cheryl. *What was going on?*

"Lacey, Cheryl," Trent began, "Shane and I have done a lot of thinking and talking over the last few weeks while he's been in the hospital, and we've made a decision." He gestured towards Daddy to pick up.

"You know what I've always said, kiddo. About taking each day as it comes, but making it count?"

I nodded.

"Well, what with the hurricane and my little stint in the hospital, it made us realize that if we have happiness right in front of us, what are waiting for? Cheryl, you'll forgive me if I don't kneel," Daddy added and movement from the corner of my eye brought my attention back to Trent, who was kneeling at my side.

"Lacey," he said at the same time as Daddy addressed Cheryl, "I love you, and I love Candace like she's my own. I can't not act on that any longer. Marry me, Lacey. Let me adopt Candy and make you two my family, please?"

I couldn't breathe while he opened a velvet box and presented me with a ring. The setting was platinum, with a large round cut diamond in the center flanked by two smaller round emeralds. The band itself was channel set with smaller diamonds.

On the other side of the table, Cheryl had already accepted Daddy's proposal, which I'd missed, enraptured by Trent's as I was. All eyes had turned back to us, Rebecca and Candy's the brightest and most excited. They sported huge smiles on their faces, and Rebecca looked like she might cry.

"So, Lacey, are you going to make me the happiest man on earth?" Trent asked, taking the ring from its plush bed and reaching for my left hand. I glanced at Candy to find her nodding her head with fervor and bouncing in her spot, her body language telling me she was more than willing to accept. I swear I even felt a small flutter in my stomach, though I knew it was much too soon.

"Yes." I smiled down at him. "On one condition. I want a Christmas wedding."

"What do you think, Lacey? Up or down?" Cheryl asked with her hands buried in Candy's hair, drawing me from my memories of a month ago. Nobody had questioned my request for the wedding to happen so soon; Trent had been enthusiastic in his agreement, and everyone had been ready to start planning our nuptials. Cheryl and Daddy were taking it a little bit slower, though not much. Their wedding was in the planning stages now, their sights on an early spring marriage once he was freed from having to use the walker. Unbeknownst to them, it would be perfect timing for them to go on their honeymoon and still get back before the baby was born, since I was due in late May.

For once, I was thankful that I had a curvy enough frame that, while it was obvious I had put on a little weight, no one could tell it was baby-induced yet. We were just letting everyone assume my added pounds were because I was less stressed and eating with regularity again. While the news had been kept a secret from everyone else, I had stood by my decision to tell Trent after we'd gone to bed on Thanksgiving. I owed him an explanation for why I wanted a Christmas wedding, not to mention that he just deserved to know. When I'd thought he'd be pleased, I'd underestimated him—ecstatic and over the moon had been more like it.

We'd celebrated our engagement and the baby news by consummating our love again at long last.

"I'm not sure. What do you want, short stuff?"

"As long as I can wear the special headband, I don't care." Candy smiled at the two of us. We were going with a Christmas theme: red, white, and silver for the colors; poinsettias and evergreens for the flowers. We'd found a headband for Candy with two silver poinsettias perched to the side; I knew it was going to be beautiful against her dark hair.

"In that case, how about down so it helps keep your shoulders warm?" I suggested, thinking of her flower girl dress with its spaghetti straps.

She shrugged, agreeing with a, "Sounds good to me," and Cheryl set to work with the large-barreled curling iron, layering her hair with big fluffy curls.

I tried not to fidget in my chair. The ladies from JJ's, the local beauty salon, had come out to the house to make me pretty. Judy was busy with my nails, giving me an acrylic French manicure with silver tips, while Jackie was putting the finishing touches on my makeup.

"Did you get the cake finished last night?" Rebecca asked from her chair next to me, where her hair was being fixed.

I grinned and nodded. "It came out better than I expected. Thank you so much for the ideas for it."

In keeping with the theme, she had suggested we go with a square, tiered cake. Each red velvet layer was covered in white fondant, dusted with silver, and finished off with red fondant strips laid over the top to give the appearance of ribbons on a package. The hardest part had been the poinsettias that nestled against the corners of the layers. As the flower was poisonous to a degree, I couldn't have the real thing on the cake, so I'd made them from gum paste. While Ms. York from the school had been a lifesaver and taken on the job of catering, the cake was my area of specialty, and I'd put my foot down that no one else would be baking it.

"How were the final details for the yard?" I asked Rebecca in return. Trent had wanted the task of organizing the venue, and I'd agreed as long as he let his mom help him. They'd checked in with me throughout the planning stages, and I was anxious to see the final result. All I knew for certain was that right now while the women were getting ready, the men were turning the back lawn into a tented winter wonderland with lots of space heaters.

All too soon, it was time to put on the dress. Candy dressed first and then stood by in her ankle length, apple-red, satin gown. It had a thin white sash around the waist, which tied in a bow at the back. In her hands she held a small basket: white with embroidered, red scrollwork and filled with holiday potpourri. We took a few minutes, making sure my tears at the sight of her hadn't ruined my makeup. My little girl was becoming a young woman, a quite beautiful one at that.

Once my dress was on and zipped up, there was a collective gasp from the room. It was strapless, the bodice an apple red with white embroidery around the waist and along the top edge. The bodice met the satin of the skirt, which cascaded down in a white waterfall, enhanced by the petticoat I wore beneath it but also hiding the slight bump that now showed when I was bare.

Candy had come forward to give me a hug, whispering how pretty she thought I looked, when there was a knock on the door. Daddy poked his head in, my white and red poinsettia bouquet with blue spruce fronds in his hand. "Showtime, kiddo."

~oOo~

Had a full month already passed since I asked her to be mine? Yes, it had, and it'd been crazy. What was new?

However, none of it mattered now as I stood in my designated spot, off to the side of the red cloth we'd rolled over the ground to create the main aisle between the guests' seating. Lacey was about to become my wife. The paperwork had already been filed to start the adoption process on Candy. If those things weren't enough to plant me firmly in the land of satisfaction, the fact that Lacey was also carrying my child would have done it. I hadn't stopped grinning since she'd shared the news with me the night I'd proposed. At first I thought I'd misheard her, and she'd had to repeat the words: "Trent, we're having a baby. Your son or daughter is growing inside me." I'd bawled like a baby, shedding tears of happiness while I made love to my fiancée.

To distract myself for my last few minutes as a single man, I ran through my to-do list. The heaters were warming the dining tent. The tables all had their holly berry and pine centerpieces. For seating, the folding chairs had been covered in white with red sashes and finished with more of the holly berries and pine attached to the bows in the back. The buffet table was decked out with sprigs of blue spruce, into which the assorted dishes had been tucked. Ms. York had been cooking up a storm for the occasion. Candy had insisted on a *hors d'oeuvre* tower, and I had to give her credit—it looked great in the middle of the table.

To begin, the band was arranged in the ceremony tent, creating a soft, pleasing background sound while we waited. They would move to the dining tent, which included a temporary dance floor, after the ceremony. Shane would be standing up as my Best Man, moving to my side after he walked Lacey down the aisle. Adjusting my boutonnière – a red, ribbon-wrapped stem below white and silver foliage with a splash of holly berries – I heard the first notes of Mendelssohn's wedding march and looked up as all the guests stood.

Candace appeared first, looking more a lady than ever. Her outfit was perfect: mature without being too much, giving her that edge that said she's wasn't a little girl anymore. She wore a dazzling smile that stretched ear-to-ear as she strode towards me with confidence, walking on her tiptoes in her sparkling red flats and tossing potpourri along the way. I gave her a wink when she got close and took her place on the other side as Lacey's Maid of Honor.

The crescendo in the music made me look back up the aisle. I had time to take a deep breath before it rushed out of me when Shane and Lacey came into view. Tears gathered in the corner of my eyes at the knowledge that it was not just my bride walking towards me, but my future family as well.

My future.

When Shane placed Lacey's hand in mine, I took it with pride, and we turned to face the minister. I couldn't tell you what words he said; I was lost in Lacey's green eyes the whole time and had to be prompted to repeat my parts back.

My trance was broken when he pronounced us man and wife and told me to kiss my bride. The afternoon festivities began when he uttered the best words I'd ever heard:

"Ladies and gentlemen, may I present Mr. and Mrs. Childress."

Epilogue

Candace is a Smart Cookie

Watching my parents kiss under the archway decorated with mistletoe, my smile grew even wider. Silly Mom thought I hadn't noticed how tight her clothes had been getting. I wasn't stupid; I could count, and I understood where babies came from. The smile on my face was there not only because I knew her secret, but also because I had one of my own:

If you want something bad enough – a family – and you wish on it hard enough when you blow out your candles, birthday wishes do come true.

Or at least that was what I was going to tell myself.

~The End~

R.E. Hargrave

About the Author

R.E. Hargrave lives on the outskirts of Dallas, TX where she prides herself on being a domestic engineer. Married to her high school sweetheart, together they are raising three children from elementary age to college age. She is an avid reader, a sometimes quilter and now, a writer. Other hobbies include gardening and a love of a music.

Her works include:

Haunted Raine, a novella

To Serve is Divine, Book One in The Divine Trilogy

A Divine Life, Book Two in The Divine Trilogy

www.rehargrave.com

Sugar & Spice

© **2013 R.E. Hargrave**